I know this to be true

Jacinda Ardern

on kindness,
empathy &
strength

Interview and photography
Geoff Blackwell

murdoch books
Sydney | London

in association with

Blackwell&Ruth.

Dedicated to the legacy
and memory of
Nelson Mandela

'What if we no longer see ourselves based on what we look like, what religion we practice, or where we live, but by what we value? Humanity. Kindness. An innate sense of our connection to each other. And a belief that we are guardians, not just of our home and our planet, but of each other. We are borderless, but we can be connected. We are inherently different, but we have more that we share.'

Introduction

Jacinda Ardern never expected to be prime minister. Growing up in the sleepy town of Murupara in a rural part of New Zealand's North Island, population 3,000, her childhood was spent driving tractors, docking sheep and picking fruit from the family orchard. She had a pet lamb called Reggie, whom she attempted (unsuccessfully) to train for the community A&P (Agricultural & Pastoral) show. Her parents were hardworking and down-to-earth; her father was a policeman and her mother worked at the school café.

When the family moved north to the Bay of Plenty, she first bore witness to the inequality present in New Zealand. 'I always noticed when things felt unfair. Of course, when you're a kid, you don't call it social justice. I just thought it was wrong that other kids didn't have what I had,' she says.[1] Outside of her studies and part-time job at the local fish and chip shop, she began to join human rights groups at school and push for change. An early act involved campaigning for girls to be permitted to wear long pants as part of the uniform at her secondary school, Morrinsville College. She won.

Despite her early engagement with politics, Ardern initially viewed it more as a side-interest than a potential profession. 'When I eventually signed up to a political party when I was seventeen, I wasn't looking for a career. I wanted, perhaps naively, to change the world.'[2] Fast-forward twenty years to her swearing-in as the fortieth prime minister of New Zealand and it's clear that she has not only established a definitive career in politics, but is well on track to creating fundamental changes.

As the world's youngest female head of government, Ardern was hailed by many as a champion for women's rights. An advocate for gender equality, she has long taken a strong stance against policies and rhetoric that discriminate against women. Before she was elected, she openly challenged a radio host who posited that employers have the right to ask females if they plan to have children when hiring new staff. 'It is totally unacceptable in 2017 to say that women should have to answer that question in the workplace,' she argued. 'It is the woman's decision about when they choose to have children. It should not predetermine whether or not they get the job.'[3]

Three months into her first term as prime minister, she announced that she and long-term partner Clarke Gayford were expecting their first child. When she returned to full ministerial duties six weeks after giving birth, critics questioned how she would manage the dual roles of new mother and prime minister, while supporters proclaimed her to be a role model for women. To both, Ardern simply pointed out that there were countless women who juggled careers and motherhood – and unlike most, she had extra help. 'I am lucky, I have an incredible support network around me. I have the ability to take my child to work – there's not many places you can do that. I am not the gold standard for bringing up a child in this current environment, because there are things about my circumstances that are not the same.'[4]

But it isn't just gender equality that Ardern has consistently lobbied for. Throughout her time in government she has worked to ensure that all people – regardless of their gender, race or age – don't just have equal opportunities, but are treated with the same level of respect. No more clearly was this shown than in the aftermath of the March 2019 mosque shootings in Christchurch, New Zealand.[i] With genuine empathy and compassion, she offered condolences and comfort to those affected both directly and indirectly by the attacks, and assured New Zealanders that what had happened was not a reflection of the country's inclusive values. 'They were New Zealanders. They are us. And because they are us, we, as a nation, mourn them,' she said.[5] In the same breath, she condemned the attacker, while refusing to use his name, and moved to introduce stricter gun laws.

Acting efficiently is a strength of Ardern's, who progresses issues and takes direct involvement with the projects that she believes are most important for the country — be it reducing child poverty and homelessness or improving the mental health system and combatting climate change. A long-time proponent of reducing national carbon emissions, she wasted no time in introducing the Green Investment Fund, investing in low-emission transportation, mitigating agricultural emissions, ending new offshore oil and gas explorations, and undertaking research about renewable energy. Part of her Government's commitment to address climate change and support New Zealand's transition towards a net-zero-emissions economy, it was a precursor to landmark climate legislation passed by New Zealand Parliament in November 2019[ii] that aims to reduce the country's carbon emissions to zero by 2050 and meet its commitments under the Paris climate accords.[iii] 'I still remember as a candidate, over ten years ago, being booed when I talked about climate change,' she recalls. 'We have to hear the anxiety that young people feel when they see the consequences – the very real images – of climate change around them. Our job is to give them hope, not just in words but in action, and we also have to give certainty.'[6]

Politics aside, Ardern is at once practical, genuine and easily relatable. Not afraid to show she's human, she has publicly shared her personal interests, as well as the more private aspects of her life. From her short-lived foray into DJ'ing and her love of pets (her cat, Paddles, was a social media star), to her relationship with her partner Gayford and her experience as a mother, she has never shied away from openly discussing what life outside the Beehive is like.[iv] In a nutshell, Ardern is an example of a progressive, modern leader with a vision centred around equality and the drive to achieve it. But on a deeper level, she shows that it's possible to govern with kindness, integrity and common sense, embracing diversity and unity, all while remaining authentic, modest and grounded.

'Imagine a country in which everyone is earning, learning, caring or volunteering. That's the kind of place that breeds happiness.'

Prologue

*Ko nga tangata katoa, e manaakitia ana te
whenua, o te Ao Whanui
Ko nga kaitiaki, e riterite ana, nga whenua,
huri rauna, i te Ao
Me tu tatou ki te werohia i nga wero
I te ingoa o te tika o nga mea katoa
Tena koutou katoa*

To all those who care for the lands of the
wide world
To the guardians of sustainability
around the world
Stand and challenge the challenges
In the name of what is right with all things
Greetings to you all

Friends,

I greet you in te reo Māori, language of the
tangata whenua, or first people, of Aotearoa
New Zealand.

I do so not just because it is the same way
I would begin an address if I were at home,
but because there are challenges we face as a
world that I know no better way to express.

Māori concepts like *kaitiakitanga*. The idea
that each of us here today are guardians.

Guardians of the land, of our environment and of our people.

There is a simplicity to the notion of sovereign guardianship.

For decades we have assembled here under the assumption that we narrowly cooperate only on the issues that overtly impact on one another; issues like international trade rules, the law of the sea, or humanitarian access to war zones.

The space in between has essentially been left to us.

We, the political leaders of the world, have been the authors of our own domestic politics and policies. Decisions have been our own, and we have lived with the consequences.

But the world has changed.

Over time we have become increasingly interdependent. We see more and more often domestic decisions that have global ramifications.

Physical events have taught us that in obvious ways: oil spills that show no respect for maritime boundaries; nuclear accidents and testing, the impacts of which are never confined to the exact location in which they occur.

But our interdependence, our connection, runs so much deeper than that, and experiences in recent years should lead us to all question whether any of us ever truly operate in isolation anymore.

This is a question that we, the remote but connected nation of New Zealand, have been grappling with this year.

There are things that we in New Zealand are well known for. Green rolling hills, perfect you might say for hobbits to hide and for plenty of sheep to roam.

We're known for *manaakitanga*, or the pride we take in caring for our guests, so much so that it even extends to our most entrenched sporting rivals.

And now we are known for something else.

The fifteenth of March 2019.

The day an alleged terrorist undertook the most horrific attack on a place of worship, taking the lives of fifty-one innocent people, devastating our Muslim community and challenging our sense of who we are as a country.

There is no changing a nation's history, but we can choose how it defines us.

And in Aotearoa New Zealand, the people
who lined up outside of mosques with flowers,
the young people who gathered spontaneously
in parks and open spaces in a show of solidarity,
the thousands who stopped in silence to
acknowledge the call to prayer seven days later,
and the Muslim community who showed only
love – these are the people who collectively
decided that New Zealand would not be
defined by an act of brutality and violence,
but instead by compassion and empathy.

Make no mistake though, we do not
claim to be a perfect nation.

While we are home to more than two
hundred ethnicities, that does not mean
we are free from racism and discrimination.
We have wounds from our own history that,
two hundred and fifty years on from the first
encounters between Māori and Europeans,
we continue to address.

But since the terrorist attack in New
Zealand, we have had to ask ourselves many
hard and difficult questions.

One example sticks in my mind.

It was only days after the shooting and
I visited a mosque in our capital city. After

spending some time with community leaders I exited and walked across the car park where members of the Muslim community were gathered.

Out of the corner of my eye I saw a young boy gesture to me.

He was shy, almost retreating towards a barrier, but he also had something he clearly wanted to say. I quickly crouched down next to him.

He didn't say his name or even say hello, he simply whispered, 'Will I be safe now?'.

What does it take for a child to feel safe?

As adults, we are quick to make the practical changes that will enable us to say that such a horrific act could never happen again. And we did that.

Within ten days of the attack we made a decision to change our guns laws and banned military-style semi-automatic weapons and assault rifles in New Zealand.

We have started on a second tranche of reforms to register weapons and change our licensing regime.

These changes will help to make us safer.

But when you're a child, fear is not

discrete, and it cannot be removed through legislative acts or decrees from Parliament.

Feeling safe means the absence of fear.

Living free from racism, bullying and discrimination. Feeling loved, included and able to be exactly who you are.

And to feel truly safe, those conditions need to be universal. No matter who you are, no matter where you come from, no matter where you live.

The young Muslim boy in Kilbirnie, New Zealand, wanted to know if I could grant him all of those things.

My fear is, that as a leader of a proudly independent nation, this is one thing I cannot achieve alone. Not anymore.

In our borderless and technologically connected world, commentary on race, acts of discrimination based on religion, gender, sexuality or ethnicity – they are not neatly confined behind boundaries. They are felt globally.

The fact I received so many letters from Muslim children from around the world in the weeks after March fifteen speaks to the power of connection.

These children had no sense of distance.
They may have never heard of New Zealand
before March fifteen. They just saw an act
of hatred against their community, and it
felt close to them.

Whether it is acts of violence, language
intended to incite fear of religious groups,
or assumptions about ethnicities to breed
distrust and racism – these actions and
utterances are as globalized as the movement
of goods and services.

Children hear them.

Women hear them.

People of faith hear them.

Our rainbow communities hear them.

And so now, it's our turn to stop
and to listen.

From an address to the United Nations General Assembly, September 2019

The Interview

Tell us a little about yourself.

My name is Jacinda Ardern and I'm the prime minister of New Zealand. And I'm the third female prime minister, the second youngest, and the youngest female prime minister.

What really matters to you, particularly in your role as a leader?

People drive everything that I do, everything that I've ever been motivated to do and I think that even when you've got some of the most challenging, difficult problems or you're looking to take on the most challenging or difficult roles, if it's all centred around the thing that motivates you the most in the world, then you'll be surprised what you can do and what you can overcome. So, for me, the fact that I do a job that is so centred on people, that's what keeps me going.

What were the seeds of that? Did you have
a particular ambition or aspiration as a young
person? Where did this idea about caring about
other people come from?

I just can always remember being a pretty
angsty child. I worried about people around
me; I noticed if children around me didn't
have what I had; I've very clear memories of
living in a very small town in New Zealand
that went through a pretty tough period, and
my dad was the local policeman there. So we
moved to this little town of 3,000 people and
I vividly remember when kids didn't have food
to eat at school. I remember walking home
one day and seeing a little boy in the middle
of winter who just didn't have any shoes.
And things like that really raised so many
questions for me, so I think in large part it was
just part of who I was, but otherwise I also
learned a huge amount from my parents. To
this day people ask me who my role models
are and of all of the world leaders that I could
possibly choose, I still choose my mother and
my father. My mother was just, for me, the
epitome of kindness; if she saw anyone in
need around us she'd be the first person to

bake a casserole or whip up a cake. That was just the kind of person she was. So, in part, I probably got that angstiness from her.

Has there been a special individual or individuals that have particularly inspired you by their example or wisdom?

Yes, yes, yes! I've always been fascinated by people who endure, you know? Who, instead of choosing an easier road with their lives, choose to take on these enormous challenges, and it's why I think people like Nelson Mandela, but also people like Ernest Shackleton, who just choose to take that path less travelled, and even though it comes with such adversity, keep going and bring people with them. That for me is incredible.

You were seventeen when you joined the Labour Party?

Yes, I joined a political party when I was a teenager and for me it wasn't because I thought a life in politics was for me. Absolutely no! In fact, if anything, I thought it looked like a very hard life. It was because I was one of those young people that thought I'd like to change the world, even if it was in the smallest of ways, it just felt like I was doing something that would make a difference. So, in amongst my job of working at a supermarket as a check-out girl, I wanted something that felt a bit more meaningful, and even if that was just delivering flyers, or knocking on doors, that was enough for me to make me feel like I was doing something useful. So I probably could have joined a political party a lot earlier than that! But, you know, it set me on a path I didn't expect.

At seventeen did you imagine ever that you would become prime minister?

Until the day before I became prime minister I couldn't have imagined becoming prime minister! And in part that's because I'm a New Zealander and we are naturally quite a self-deprecating people, and part, if I'm honest, it's probably because I'm also a women who looks more quickly at my deficits; the things that I'm not good at, rather than what I am.

But either way, I never would have imagined as a child that I would end up doing a role like this, because I grew up in a very small town, and there are one hundred and twenty MPs (members of Parliament) in New Zealand. How could I possibly imagine being one of them?

You've become an internationally famous person, a role model for many around the world, but it was just over three years ago that the then-leader of the Labour Party called you into his office and said, 'I don't think I can get there,' and said that he wanted to place his trust in you. I remember that first press conference . . .

So do I!

. . . the impact you made, and the authority and confidence you brought to that moment. I think many people around New Zealand felt that perhaps you didn't have enough experience, or that you were too young. What gave you the confidence to suddenly step forward?

You're absolutely right. It was my birthday when the leader of the political party that I was then deputy leader of, said to me,

'I don't think I can get the numbers up in order for us to win the election.'[v] It was seven weeks away and I remember being absolutely adamant [saying], 'You have to stay.' I thought we needed to be consistent and that people wouldn't appreciate us losing a leader so close to an election, but he'd made his mind up. And at that point I thought, 'Well, he's decided, now I just need to get on with it.' There wasn't a question in my mind that now I had a job to do and that I could do it. You know it's one thing to not be able to necessarily imagine yourself in that position, but when you're there you're just actually thinking, 'Right, there's no time for me to second-guess myself now, people don't need to hear me question anything right now, they just need to know, and hear me say, "I can."' And so, in that moment, I absolutely knew I could and so it was just a matter of going out there and showing that.

You've talked about that moment in terms of trusting your instincts. Was that something you trusted before you got into this?

Yes. I don't know what I would do in this role or in politics without having instincts that I trust. Now that doesn't mean that I choose to ignore evidence and research – that's very, very important to me, to make evidence-informed decisions – but actually you just can't ignore what your instincts are telling you; nor should you. I think one of the dangers of leadership now, and particularly in politics, is that we have so much information now, and so much research around the way that people think, and the way they process what they hear, and how we're meant to present ourselves, that you run the risk of becoming over-engineered. And I think, if there's anything that people need right now, is they just need to see human beings doing their best as leaders. And that means that from time to time you'll stumble, and you should be honest about that; it means that people will see your failings and we should be honest about that too. People need authenticity, not, I think, some manufactured idea of what political leadership is meant to be. And so, I feel lucky that, because I only had seven weeks, all I could be was myself. And that's all I've ever tried to be. And if that means I'm successful on behalf of New Zealand, that's great, and if it means that I'm not, then I'll still sleep at night.

What is instinct for you? Is it a combination of head and heart?

Yes, it's very hard for me to describe, but I've seen people who've lost trust in their instinct; I've seen what happens when you don't follow it any more; and I've certainly had times where I haven't listened to it and I've learned the lesson of that as well. It's just . . . if a proposition is put to you – and the easiest way I can describe it is if you're really struggling with a decision and you think, 'OK, I'm going to fall on this side of it, this is what I'm going to do', and you still feel unsettled – if it just doesn't sit with you, then maybe it means you've fallen on the wrong side of it. So I always just teach myself, sit with it for a little bit and if it's still not squaring, then I know to go in the other direction.

If you were to summarize the qualities that have underpinned your path to this leadership role, that you think have been most important for you?

Kindness, and not being afraid to be kind, or to focus on, or be really driven by empathy. I think one of the sad things that I've seen in political leadership is – because we've placed over time so much emphasis on notions of assertiveness and strength – that we probably have assumed that it means you can't have those other qualities of kindness and empathy. And yet, when you think about all the big challenges that we face in the world, that's probably the quality we need the most. We need our leaders to be able to empathize with the circumstances of others; to empathize with the next generation that we're making decisions on behalf of. And if we focus only on being seen to be the strongest, most powerful person in the room, then I think we lose what we're meant to be here for. So I'm proudly focussed on empathy, because you can be both empathetic and strong.

Do you have guiding principles or a driving
philosophy that you fall back on in tough times?

I think probably the easiest way for me to
capture it is I am so driven by people, I'm
driven by empathy, but I want to make lasting
change. In politics, particularly politics when
you're in a very small country, you know that
within five minutes of leaving, that's your
time gone. People eventually won't remember
who you were or what your name was – and
actually none of that matters – but if the
things that you did, on behalf of other people,
if they've endured, then you know you've
made a difference. Then you know you've
been successful. I still remember the first
time I stood in Parliament, we have a tradition
that if a Member of Parliament passes away,
even after they've left office, we'll stand
and we'll have a moment's silence. And I'm
fairly engaged in politics and know a lot of
people who have passed through, but I still
remember the first time we stood up for a
name I didn't know, and I thought, 'It won't be
long where everyone's legacy leaves,' but if
you know you've made a difference on climate

change or for poverty, then that's actually something to feel proud of. Who cares if they don't know who the person was who did it?

Do you have daily disciplines or routines that you practice?

Probably my daily disciplines are more centred around what I don't do, rather than what I do! So, particularly in this modern era where there's a real intensity to leadership now that I just don't think existed even ten years ago – the judgement is swift and it's constant and it can come from all angles, particularly in the social media age, and we have to carry on, regardless. We just have to keep going, and so my advice is: Know when you don't feel tough enough to take it from every angle, from all sides, and just check out of some of those spaces if you need to. Give yourself breathing room because there will always be those who will be detractors of what you do. And just know when you're not tough enough to face that.

What qualities have been most critical to enable you to survive in that space, and to achieve the goals you are setting for yourself?

Do you know, actually I think it's really important to acknowledge that sometimes there aren't great days. I think we want our leaders to be humans, we want more and more people who are reflective of our societies and communities to decide to run in politics, and I think the worst thing we can do for them is pretend that it's easy or that actually we are superheroes and we can do everything – be in politics and be parents, and be daughters and sisters, and be fabulous at all of those things. I think that will just alienate people because how can they see themselves in those roles unless we actually say, 'Hmm, you know actually, some days it's tough, I need a lot of help, I have a great mother and father, and in-laws who do lots for me.' And then people can go, 'Ah, okay, so I can do that, I just need a community around me.' That's the reality, so I'm very quick not to say that there's a perfect way to do things or this magic bit of mindfulness or meditation will get you through. Some of the days are hard, but some of them are just fabulous as well.

Was yesterday, when the New Zealand Parliament passed the Zero Carbon Amendment Bill, one of those special days?

I think so, alongside the legislation we passed a year ago on child poverty. I've always said that if I can leave politics having made a difference on child poverty and climate change, I'd feel like I'd left something behind that was worthwhile. And so the other key factor for me is to make it last, bring people with you. Those important legacies of people like Nelson Mandela, and some of the people that I've admired, they all worked really hard to try and build a movement, and so what was equally important was that that law passed yesterday unopposed. And with our child poverty legislation only one person voted against it. That says to me it'll last, and that's critical.

What are the biggest lessons you've learned as a leader?

That you won't necessarily get tougher. When I first came into politics I remember talking to a Member of Parliament who I thought was quite a tough cookie, and asking him, 'How did you, how do you, build your thick skin?'. He was horrified that I thought that he was like that! He said stuff still got to him, and that actually if stuff ever stopped getting to you then you'd probably lost your empathy, and it was never worth losing that. And so, I actually decided I didn't necessarily want to build some tough exterior. Instead I just learned how to filter things; how to kind of take on board that criticism and listen to it when I needed to, or otherwise say, 'Well, actually that person's just coming from a very different perspective', and just learn how to filter it. And so that was a really big learning curve, you know? Actually, the world doesn't need a whole lot of massively thick-skinned politicians; they *do* need people who care. The odd sensitive flower is okay.

Are there moments where you just feel hurt?

Oh yes, every day. But I don't hold onto grievance; if you just went around in politics collecting grievance and grudges, the only person that's going to end up hurting is yourself. You need to just get on with it. I'm no saint, I get irritated, I get annoyed – and then I move on.

Can you describe a key moment or crisis that has particularly tested you as a leader?

Yes, the fifteenth of March [2019]. That was when New Zealand, for the first time in its modern history, experienced a horrific terrorist attack in the Muslim community. Fifty-one people lost their lives.

Tell us a little about your process and feelings
around that time. How did you work out how
you, as a leader, were supposed to react?
What you could do?

You know, I don't ever remember thinking
about how I was meant to react or what it
was I was meant to be. The only thing I did
remember thinking, was that I knew I couldn't
show every emotion that I was feeling; that
wasn't what everyone needed. They really
just wanted to hear what everyone else was
thinking. I've always said I felt like all I did at
that time was just reflect back what I was
seeing, and amongst this horrific human
tragedy I just saw this outpouring of grief
and love for a community who gave that all
back in return. And that was one of the things
I think to this day remains the most staggering
for me in all of this, that not even twenty-four
hours after the shooting I went to Christchurch
and sat face to face with some of the people
who, the day before, were in the media
covered in blood having been right there
where this massacre occurred, and as they
stood up I just couldn't imagine what they
were going to say. I thought it might be anger,

but they stood and said, 'Thank you'. They thanked New Zealanders. Twenty-four hours later they were thanking us for our response to the community, and that was both devastating and also had me in awe; that a community could be so forgiving. And so really, from there, that just said to me, 'Well, who are we to display anything other than love and kindness under those circumstances', and that's what New Zealand did.

The natural but concerted effort you made to show real support and love for the Muslim community resonated with Muslims all around the world. Was it an instinctive decision to wear a hijab?

I don't actually ever remember making a decision, I just remember focusing on how soon I could get down there, that one of the issues was that it took us a little while to determine the extent of the attack, whether or not there were any wider safety issues for the police before I could go down there. And so that's where the focus was – 'How quickly can I get there?'. And then as soon as I knew

I could, I just phoned a friend – because
I wasn't in my home, I was then unexpectedly
in Wellington – and just said, 'Please can
I borrow a scarf'. So I don't remember making
any of those decisions and that's probably one
of my reflections around leadership generally:
If we give ourselves a moment just to be
who we are, then many of these things just
become intuitive. And I'd say to anyone that
if you were in that circumstance of being
face to face with people who had lost loved
ones and members of their community, and
you're face to face with their grief, you'd reach
out and embrace them too. It's just who we
are as humans. I just think we need to stop
second-guessing ourselves sometimes.

Once again, did it just came naturally to follow
your instincts at that moment?

What else are you left with? When you've
got in front of you an experience that you
just can't even fathom New Zealand having,
sometimes that's all you're left with.

Did you understand the impact you had not only
on your fellow New Zealanders, but the impact
you were having on the world?

No, not at the time. It didn't really hit home to
me, I guess, because actually being a small
country, we were very hands on. We were
meeting three times a day, sorting through the
logistical details of making sure everyone was
safe – that families were being reunified, that
we were bringing in families from offshore –
there was a lot of practical work to be done.
And I was trying to really craft gun legislation
very, very quickly as well. So, to be honest,
I didn't think much outside of what we were
doing for quite some weeks. So it was much,
much later that I really reflected on any of that,
but not at the time.

How do you deal with mistakes you've made?

Oh, I dwell on them for ages! I really punish
myself, I kick myself, so yes, not well actually!
Not well at all.

And endeavours that have failed? What's your process as a prime minister in a world where you're apparently not allowed to make mistakes?

Yes. I don't have any tips here . . . if I make a mistake I really punish myself over it – I really feel like I've let people down – so actually for me it's more about what I do to get over that so that I can just actually still be productive and get on with things. So the best tip I can offer is just talking to people; talking to people who understand, who have been there, who just help me move past it.

What do you think the world needs more of?

Just humans being humans, just finding our humanity again. Of course we're a world full of diversity and we are full of difference, be it ethnic or cultural or religious, but actually in those moments of deep pain, in those moments of tragedy when you strip it all back, we all have a shared humanity and we just need to remember that more often. I think it changes our view of the world and the way that we try and do things if we just remember

that, in amongst all of the difference,
that exists.

What does leadership mean to you?

I've changed my view of it over time. When
I was younger I probably would have given
you a description of leadership that was
completely different to the one I'd give you
now. And I'd give you a whole lot of character
traits of things that I'd just observed.

What were they?

When I was younger I probably would have
said things like 'assertive' and 'bold' and
'courageous' and 'out in front', and maybe a bit
'domineering'. Just the things that you might
have witnessed a decade, or two decades,
or three decades ago in politics. Now I think
actually leaders don't necessarily have to be at
the front of the pack; they can be in the middle
of rallying people, motivating them, finding new
leaders. I think leaders come in many different
forms now, and they're in our communities,
and they are in our homes and, sometimes,

they're quiet and unassuming, but they leave a legacy, and they leave a mark on our lives.

Listening, has that become an important part of your leadership?

Yes, yes, absolutely. More than listening, really *hearing* someone. I think probably one of the things I missed the most for a while was that in our system it's very easy to be close to the ground, and to where people are feeling the impact of things when they go wrong, and I always try and find ways to stay close to that.

Gender has been a focus for you. What would you say to young women around the world?

I don't want to make assumptions or grand assertions, but at least in my experience there are two issues that women almost always universally face. One is that there are very literal barriers to leadership and some of them will be just blatant sexism. Some of it will be barriers because of the multiple roles that women have being carers as well as leaders in their workplaces; these are literal. And all of that we have a role in doing something about. But then there's another barrier, and that is that I do see a confidence gap with our women, and it can start really, really young. I've gone to schools a lot and I'll often ask young women to write down the thing, that if you can do anything in the world, you would like to do. And I'll give them all a little bit of time to do that and then I'll say, 'Okay, now write down what you think you're *going* to do', and without hesitation you see them go straight back, you know, writing that next thing. The fact that we have young people who are so quick to immediately assume that they won't do the thing that they aspire to do makes me deeply sad, but I also totally understand because I wouldn't have ever written 'prime minister' as my first thing. I wouldn't have even fathomed it, let alone even contemplating being a Member of Parliament. So I reflect on why that is for myself in order to try and convince others that we can't let ourselves become a barrier; there are enough barriers in this world without ourselves being one of them as well.

Where do you get that confidence?

I don't know, necessarily. I actually don't think that there was some big moment where I suddenly found confidence, I found responsibility instead. And that actually has always been a bigger motivation for me, more than anything else; that sense of duty. I had opportunities where people would come to me and say, 'We think you should do this'. And I think, 'Ooh, I don't know that I'm up for that', but then I'd feel like I had to, that I owed it to people, I owed it to others who are asking me, that I had a duty, a responsibility. That in the end was what overcame my confidence gap; feeling like I needed to for other people. And look, whatever it takes. It was the right thing for me.

What coping mechanisms did you utilize when you encountered that blatant sexism you refer to?

You know, actually, I would be doing a disservice to New Zealand if I didn't acknowledge that relative to others, my experience has been pretty good. I still have stories to tell, but compared to some of the things I've heard and read, it doesn't compare. And I can, in large part, lay that at the feet of the women who've been in politics before me. The fact that I can be the third female prime minister means there'll be a generation now who's known two female and one male prime minister, so I almost feel like I have stories, but I don't really have grievance in the way others rightly do.

There's a little quiet voice inside your head sometimes when the odd thing happens so you just think, 'I think I might show you up on that a little later'. So, yes, you just form little strategies. You just know that your time will come.

What advice would you give your twenty-year-old self?

It will be okay. Yes, it will be okay. I think I'd probably describe myself as having been a bit of an angsty anxious young person with a lot to do and, you know, constantly worrying about whether or not you are doing enough, doing it well enough. All anyone asks, you just do your best. So, it'll be okay.

'There are so many issues we end up divided on which, if you distilled them down to a simple concept, you would find we are in fact united on.'

Epilogue

Undeniably, our sea levels are rising. Undeniably, we are experiencing extreme weather events, increasingly so. Undeniably, the science tells us the impact that there will be on flora and fauna and, yes, also the spread of diseases in areas where we previously haven't seen them. We know, as well, that some island nations will have their clean water sources impacted by rising sea levels and saltwater entering into them. On a daily basis they are already seeing those impacts. Our world is warming, and so, therefore, the question for all of us is: what side of history will we choose to sit on, in this moment in time?

I absolutely believe and continue to stand by the statement that climate change is the biggest challenge of our time, and for us here in Aotearoa New Zealand, that means that for this generation, this is our nuclear moment.[vi] And so today, if we are to truly reflect that that is what this means for us, we have to start moving beyond targets, we have to start moving beyond aspiration, we have to start moving beyond statements of hope, and deliver signs of action.

We have committed ourselves to a
1.5 degrees Celsius target that we are
embedding in legislation, not just because
of the statements of the Paris Agreement
but because that is what is required if we
are to show our Pacific neighbours that
we understand what the impacts above
1.5 degrees Celsius will have on them – it is
real. Today, we embed in legislation a Climate
Commission who will play a role in helping
us to establish carbon budgets, who will help
us establish the targets that we need across
the spectrum, that will provide for us advice,
particularly on how we deal with issues
like methane.[vii]

A nuclear-free moment needs to be
coupled with action.

There have been 170,000 New Zealanders
taking to the street, calling for that action –
not for hope but calling for that action –
around the world. I am proud at the rate at
which New Zealanders took to the street
to reinforce what it is we are doing in this
House today. I acknowledge Generation Zero.
I acknowledge all of the environmental NGOs
who have played a part for over a decade in

calling for more climate action. I acknowledge our food and fibre sector leaders, who are taking historic, bold, courageous steps on behalf of the people they represent.

When we think about climate change versus the nuclear-free moment, there are some differences, but there are some similarities, and one similarity is that a nuclear-free moment in New Zealand was something that unified us. We have to be unified in the fight against climate change. We have to move together. There will be areas where we don't always agree, and in one area it will probably be pace of change, but we will keep pushing, doing everything we can to bring you with us. But today we have made a choice that I am proud of, that will leave a legacy, and that, I hope, means the next generation will see that we in New Zealand were on the right side of history.

From an address to New Zealand Parliament, November 2019

'Leaders come in many different forms now. They're in our communities and they're in our homes, and sometimes they're quiet and unassuming but they leave a legacy and they leave a mark on our lives.'

About Jacinda Ardern

Jacinda Ardern is a New Zealand politician and Member of Parliament. In 2017 she became leader of the New Zealand Labour Party and was elected Prime Minister of New Zealand. She is the country's third female prime minister, and the country's youngest.

Ardern joined the Labour Party as a teenager, and, after finishing high school, completed a Bachelor of Communication Studies in Politics and Public Relations at the University of Waikato in Hamilton, New Zealand. After graduating, she worked in the office of then-prime minister Helen Clark before heading to London, England, where she worked as a senior policy advisor for Britain's then-prime minister Tony Blair.

Returning to New Zealand, she campaigned for a seat in Parliament and successfully entered as a list MP for the NZ Labour Party in 2008.[viii] Initially a spokesperson for Youth Affairs, she later became spokesperson for Social Development and then Justice, Children, Small Business, and Arts & Culture. In 2017, she became the MP for Auckland's Mount Albert electorate. The same year she campaigned alongside Labour Party leader Andrew Little ahead of the general election. When Little stepped down just seven weeks before the election, Ardern became leader of the Labour Party and subsequently prime minister.

A self-described social democrat, she has advocated for equal rights for all, with an emphasis on women and children. As well as prime minister, she is the current Minister for National Security and Intelligence, Minister for Arts, Culture and Heritage, and Minister for Child Poverty Reduction.

She has been acknowledged with multiple global recognitions, and was named on *TIME* magazine's '100 Most Influential People of 2019' list, and *Forbes* magazine's '25 Most Powerful Female Political Leaders of 2017' list.

She lives in New Zealand with her partner, Clarke Gayford, a television presenter and host of popular fishing documentary show *Fish of the Day*. In 2018 they welcomed their first child, Neve Te Aroha Ardern Gayford, and Ardern became only the second elected leader in the world to give birth while in office. Three months later, she made international news when she brought Gayford, who is Neve's primary caregiver, together with Neve to the United Nations General Assembly meeting in New York.

@jacindaardern

About the Project

'A true leader must work hard to ease tensions, especially when dealing with sensitive and complicated issues. Extremists normally thrive when there is tension, and pure emotion tends to supersede rational thinking.'

– Nelson Mandela

Inspired by Nelson Mandela, *I Know This to Be True* was conceived to record and share what really matters for the most inspiring leaders of our time.

I Know This to Be True is a Nelson Mandela Foundation project anchored by original interviews with twelve different and extraordinary leaders each year, for five years – six men and six women – who are helping and inspiring others through their ideas, values and work.

Royalties from sales of this book will support language translation and free access to films, books and educational programmes using material from the series, in all countries with developing economies, or economies in transition, as defined by United Nations annual classifications.

iknowthistobetrue.org

'A good head and a good
heart are always a formidable
combination.'

– Nelson Mandela

A special thanks to Jacinda Ardern, and all the generous and inspiring individuals we call leaders who have magnanimously given their time to be part of this project.

For the Nelson Mandela Foundation:
Sello Hatang, Verne Harris, Noreen Wahome, Razia Saleh and Sahm Venter

For Blackwell & Ruth:
Geoff Blackwell, Ruth Hobday, Cameron Gibb, Nikki Addison, Olivia van Velthooven, Elizabeth Blackwell, Kate Raven, Annie Cai and Tony Coombe

We hope that together we can help to mobilize Madiba's extraordinary legacy, to the benefit of communities around the world.

A note from the photographer
The photographic portraits in this book are the result of a team effort, led by Blackwell & Ruth's talented design director Cameron Gibb, who both mentored and saved this fledgling photographer. I have long harboured the desire, perhaps conceit, that I could personally create photographs for one of our projects, but through many trials, and more than a few errors, I learned that without Cameron's generous direction and sensitivity, I couldn't have come close to creating these portraits.

– Geoff Blackwell

About Nelson Mandela

Nelson Mandela was born in the Transkei, South Africa, on 18 July 1918. He joined the African National Congress in the early 1940s and was engaged in struggles against the ruling National Party's apartheid system for many years before being arrested in August 1962. Mandela was incarcerated for more than twenty-seven years, during which his reputation as a potent symbol of resistance for the anti-apartheid movement grew steadily. Released from prison in 1990, Mandela was jointly awarded the Nobel Peace Prize in 1993, and became South Africa's first democratically elected president in 1994. He died on 5 December 2013, at the age of ninety-five.

NELSON MANDELA
FOUNDATION
Living the legacy

About the Nelson Mandela Foundation

The Nelson Mandela Foundation is a non-profit organization founded by Nelson Mandela in 1999 as his post-presidential office. In 2007 he gave it a mandate to promote social justice through dialogue and memory work.

Its mission is to contribute to the making of a just society by mobilizing the legacy of Nelson Mandela, providing public access to information on his life and times and convening dialogue on critical social issues.

The Foundation strives to weave leadership development into all aspects of its work.

nelsonmandela.org

Notes

i   Terrorist shooting attacks at two mosques in Christchurch, New Zealand, on 15 March 2019, which killed fifty-one, and injured forty-nine, people.

ii   The Climate Change Response (Zero Carbon) Amendment Bill 2019 was passed by the New Zealand Parliament on 7 November 2019 to 'to provide a framework by which New Zealand can develop and implement clear and stable climate change policies that contribute to the global effort under the Paris Agreement to limit the global average temperature increase to 1.5 degrees Celsius above pre-industrial levels.'

iii   Signed in Paris, France, on 12 December 2015, the Paris Agreement builds upon the UNFCCC (United Nations Framework Convention on Climate Change) with a stated central aim to strengthen the global response to the threat of climate change by keeping a global temperature rise this century below 2 degrees Celsius, and to pursue efforts to limit the temperature increase even further to 1.5 degrees Celsius.

iv   Housing the office of the prime minister, the 'Beehive' is the common name for the Executive Wing of the New Zealand Parliament Buildings in Wellington, New Zealand, so-called because its shape is reminiscent of a type of beehive.

v   The New Zealand Labour Party (*Rōpū Reipa o Aotearoa*), known as 'Labour', a centre-left political party in New Zealand. Ardern served as deputy leader from March to August 2017, before being elected as leader.

vi   In 1984, New Zealand's then-prime minister, David Lange, barred nuclear-powered or nuclear-armed ships from entering or using New Zealand waters, and all the sea, land and airspace of New Zealand became enshrined in legislation as nuclear-free zones.

vii   See Introduction, p. 14, paragraph 2.

viii   New Zealand's electoral system is based on Mixed Member Proportional Representation (MMP). A list MP is a member of parliament who is elected from a party list rather than from a geographical constituency.

Sources and Permissions

1   Kelly Bertrand, "Jacinda Ardern's country childhood", *New Zealand Woman's Weekly*, 30 June 2014, https://www.nowtolove.co.nz/celebrity/celeb-news/jacinda-arderns-country-childhood-2894.

2   Rt. Hon. Jacinda Ardern, "Wellbeing a cure for inequality", 25 September 2019, https://www.beehive.govt.nz/speech/wellbeing-cure-inequality.

3   "Jacinda Ardern: It is 'totally unacceptable' to ask women about baby plans", *The AM Show*, Newshub, 2 August 2017, https://www.newshub.co.nz/home/election/2017/08/jacinda-ardern-it-is-totally-unacceptable-to-ask-women-about-baby-plans.html.

4   From the UNICEF 9th Annual Social Good Summit panel discussion, 24 September 2018, New York, USA.

5   Rt. Hon. Jacinda Ardern, ministerial statement, volume 737, p. 10072, 19 March 2019, https://www.parliament.nz/en/pb/hansard-debates/rhr/combined/HansD_20190319_20190319.

6   Rt. Hon. Jacinda Ardern, ministerial statement, volume 738, p. 11031, 21 May 2019, https://www.parliament.nz/en/pb/hansard-debates/rhr/document/HansS_20190521_055125000/ardern-jacinda.

The publisher is grateful for literary permissions to reproduce items subject to copyright which have been used with permission. Every effort has been made to trace the copyright holders and the publisher apologizes for any unintentional omission. We would be pleased to hear from any not acknowledged here and undertake to make all reasonable efforts to include the appropriate acknowledgement in any subsequent edition.

Pages 6, 19–25: New Zealand National Statement to United Nations General Assembly 2019, Rt. Hon. Jacinda Ardern, 25 September 2019, beehive.govt.nz/speech/new-zealand-national-statement-united-nations-general-assembly-2019; page 11: "Jacinda Ardern's country childhood", Kelly Bertrand, *New Zealand Woman's Weekly*, 30 June 2014, nowtolove.co.nz/celebrity/celeb-news/jacinda-arderns-country-childhood-2894; page 12: "Wellbeing a cure for inequality", Rt. Hon. Jacinda Ardern, 25 September 2019, beehive.govt.nz/speech/wellbeing-cure-inequality; pages 12–13: "Jacinda Ardern: It is 'totally unacceptable' to ask women about baby plans", *The AM Show*, Newshub, 2 August 2017, https://www.newshub.co.nz/home/election/2017/08/jacinda-ardern-it-is-totally-unacceptable-to-ask-women-about-baby-plans.html; page 13: UNICEF 9th Annual Social Good Summit panel discussion, 24 September 2018, New York, USA; page 14: ministerial statement, Rt. Hon. Jacinda Ardern, 19 March 2019, volume 737, p. 10072, parliament.nz/resource/en-NZ/HansD_20190319_20190319/30256f99eb599cc7196cf82ae1268ea9e4dbae84; page 15: ministerial statement, Rt. Hon. Jacinda Ardern, 21 May 2019, volume 738, p. 11031, parliament.nz/resource/en-NZ/HansD_20190521_20190521/64ae4326eb3b8e4e25c9267ecd9b0832e2604107;

pages 17, 55: Geoff Blackwell and Ruth Hobday, *200 Women: Updated and Abridged*, (Auckland, New Zealand: Blackwell & Ruth, 2018), p.34–35; pages 57–59: Address to New Zealand Parliament, November 2019, parliament.nz/en/pb/hansard-debates/rhr/combined/HansDeb_20191107_20191107_16; pages 67–68: *Nelson Mandela by Himself: The Authorised Book of Quotations* edited by Sello Hatang and Sahm Venter (Pan Macmillan: Johannesburg, South Africa, 2017), copyright © 2011 Nelson R. Mandela and the Nelson Mandela Foundation, used by permission of the Nelson Mandela Foundation, Johannesburg, South Africa.